Team Spirit®

THE OKLAHOMA CITY THUNDER

BY

MARK STEWART

Content Consultant
Matt Zeysing
Historian and Archivist
The Naismith Memorial Basketball Hall of Fame

NORWOOD HOUSE PRESS

CHICAGO, ILLINOIS

Norwood House Press
P.O. Box 316598
Chicago, Illinois 60631

For information regarding Norwood House Press, please visit our website at:
www.norwoodhousepress.com or call 866-565-2900.

All photos courtesy of Getty Images except the following:
Black Book Partners (6),
Author's Collection/Seattle SuperSonics (17, 31, 37),
Topps, Inc. (7, 9, 14, 20, 21, 29, 34 both, 35 top left & right, 38,
40 top right & bottom left, 41 top & bottom right, 43), Icon SMI (15),
Associated Press (26, 27, 28, 36, 40), The Sporting News (19),
SportsChrome (22, 35 bottom, 39, 41 left), Dexter Press (30), Matt Richman (48).
Cover photo: NBAE/Getty Images
Special thanks to Topps, Inc. and Ron Tringali

Editor: Mike Kennedy
Designer: Ron Jaffe
Project Management: Black Book Partners, LLC.
Research: Joshua Zaffos
Special thanks to Andrew Griffin and Greg Givens

Library of Congress Cataloging-in-Publication Data

Stewart, Mark, 1960-
  The Oklahoma City Thunder / by Mark Stewart ; content consultant, Matt
Zeysing.
     p. cm. -- (Team spirit)
  Includes bibliographical references and index.
  Summary: "Presents the history and accomplishments of the Oklahoma City
Thunder basketball team. Includes highlights of players, coaches, and awards,
quotes, timeline, maps, glossary and websites"--Provided by publisher.
  ISBN-13: 978-1-59953-327-8 (library edition : alk. paper)
  ISBN-10: 1-59953-327-8 (library edition : alk. paper) 1. Oklahoma City
Thunder (Basketball team)--History--Juvenile literature. 2.
Basketball--Oklahoma--Oklahoma City--History--Juvenile literature. I.
Zeysing, Matt. II. Title. z
  GV885.52.O37S74 2009
  796.323'640976638--dc22
                                                              2009012716

COVER PHOTO: Thunder fans watch the opening tip-off of the team's
first game in Oklahoma City.

Table of Contents

SPORTS WORDS & VOCABULARY WORDS: In this book, you will find many words that are new to you. You may also see familiar words used in new ways. The glossary on page 46 gives the meanings of basketball words, as well as "everyday" words that have special basketball meanings. These words appear in **bold type** throughout the book. The glossary on page 47 gives the meanings of vocabulary words that are not related to basketball. They appear in ***bold italic type*** throughout the book.

BASKETBALL SEASONS: Because each basketball season begins late in one year and ends early in the next, seasons are not named after years. Instead, they are written out as two years separated by a dash, for example 1944–45 or 2005–06.

Meet the Thunder

Anyone who has spent time in Oklahoma has heard the rumble of thunder on the horizon. The state sits between the cool, dry air of the Canadian Arctic and the warm, damp air from the Gulf of Mexico. When these forces meet over Oklahoma—and they often do—the result is a loud and violent storm.

That sound is not unlike what the Oklahoma City Thunder players hear when they take the court for a home game. In a state where college football has long been the most popular sport, fans take pleasure in the chance to make some noise for their very own **professional** basketball team.

This book tells the story of the Thunder. They are a new team in a town that was starving for basketball. They are also a team that left a basketball-hungry city behind. The Thunder face a great challenge. Win or lose, they must find new and exciting ways to link their bright future and their proud past.

Russell Westbrook and Kyle Weaver take a break during a 2008–09 game.

Way Back When

The first 41 years of the Thunder's story took place in Seattle, Washington. In 1967–68, the Seattle SuperSonics joined the **National Basketball Association (NBA)** when the league expanded from 10 to 12 teams. The other club added to the NBA was the San Diego Rockets. The "Sonics" beat the Rockets for the first win in team history.

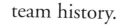

Seattle picked unwanted players from other teams, including high-scoring guard Walt Hazzard (who later converted to Islam and changed his name to Mahdi Abdul-Rahman) and a tough defender named Tom Meschery. The Sonics also **drafted** college star Bob Rule. One year later, **All-Star** Lenny Wilkens joined the team. The following season, he became Seattle's **player-coach**.

During the late 1960s and early 1970s, the NBA competed with the **American Basketball Association (ABA)**. Sonics owner Sam Schulman thought the leagues would be stronger if they *merged* into one. To get the attention of NBA owners, he threatened to move his team to Los Angeles, California and join the ABA. Eventually, the NBA agreed with Schulman, the Sonics stayed put, and the leagues joined forces for the 1976–77 season.

In the meantime, Schulman made headlines by signing the ABA's top player, Spencer Haywood. He was a lightning-quick forward who was a great scorer and rebounder. In 1971–72, Haywood led the team to its first winning season.

In 1973–74, another big name came to Seattle. **Hall of Famer** Bill Russell was signed to coach the club. Russell had won 11 championships with the Boston Celtics. He guided Seattle to a second-place finish in the **Pacific Division**. During this period, the Sonics were led by two exciting guards, "Downtown" Fred Brown and Donald "Slick" Watts. Brown was famous for his long-distance shooting. Watts specialized in defense. In their first trip to the **playoffs**, the Sonics defeated the Detroit Pistons.

LEFT: The Sonics play the San Diego Rockets during their first NBA season.
ABOVE: An autographed trading card of player-coach Lenny Wilkens.

7

A few years later, the Sonics brought Wilkens back as their coach. He rebuilt the team around a terrific backcourt—Gus Williams and Dennis Johnson—and used Brown off the bench. With the help of young centers Jack Sikma and Marvin Webster, the Sonics reached the 1978 **NBA Finals**. One year later, Seattle won its first championship.

New stars led the Sonics in the 1980s, including Dale Ellis, Tom Chambers, Nate McMillan, and Xavier McDaniel. The team's next shot at glory came in the 1990s. Coach George Karl relied on a pair of All-Stars, forward Shawn Kemp and a great **all-around** guard named Gary Payton. **Role players** Sam Perkins, Hersey Hawkins, and Detlef Schrempf filled out the **lineup**. Seattle made it back to the NBA Finals in 1995–96 but lost to Michael Jordan and the red-hot Chicago Bulls.

During their final years on the West Coast, the Sonics looked to their former star McMillan to coach the team. His **roster** featured Rashard Lewis and Ray Allen. In 2004–05, the Sonics finished first in the **Northwest Division**. It marked Seattle's sixth and final division title. In 2008, the Sonics moved to Oklahoma City and became the Thunder.

LEFT: Gary Payton and Shawn Kemp, the team's top stars during the 1990s.
ABOVE: Ray Allen fires a jump shot.

The Team Today

Running a basketball team is very expensive. The best players make millions of dollars. For a team to be successful, it must sell a lot of tickets and have a modern arena. In Seattle, the Sonics played in an old arena. Team owner Clay Bennett could not agree with the city when it came to building a new home for his club. He decided to move the Sonics to his home state of Oklahoma.

In the years before the team moved to Oklahoma City, it began to rebuild with exciting young players. In 2007, the Sonics traded Ray Allen to the Boston Celtics for Jeff Green, a talented and intelligent forward. He showed he was ready to play in the NBA the moment he stepped on the court for the team.

Green was joined by Kevin Durant, the second player chosen in the 2007 draft. Durant—who had the size and skills to play any position on the court—was named NBA **Rookie of the Year**. Durant seemed to get better and better with each game. In 2008, Oklahoma City made another smart move by drafting guard Russell Westbrook. Fans watched with great excitement as the Thunder started to build a winner around these three stars.

Kevin Durant brings the ball up the court during a 2008–09 game, with Jeff Green following close behind.

Home Court

The Thunder play their home games in an arena in downtown Oklahoma City. It looks a lot like Ford Field, the home of the Detroit Lions football team. The Thunder's arena opened in 2002. It was the home of the New Orleans Hornets for two seasons after Hurricane Katrina hit Louisiana in 2005.

During their days in Seattle, the Sonics had three homes. The team played in Seattle Center Coliseum (also known as KeyArena) from 1967 to 1978 and again from 1985 until 2008. KeyArena is located in downtown Seattle, on the site of the 1962 World's Fair. The Sonics moved to the Tacoma Dome for one season while KeyArena was being updated. From 1978 to 1985, the team played in the Kingdome, which was actually a baseball and football stadium. It was one of the NBA's noisiest arenas, and the team set many attendance records there.

BY THE NUMBERS

- *There are 19,599 seats for basketball in the Thunder's arena.*
- *It cost $89 million to build in 2002.*
- *The Thunder's arena is 586,000 square feet, which makes it the largest indoor arena in the state.*

Russell Westbrook soars high for a dunk during a 2008–09 game in the Thunder's arena.

Dressed for Success

The Thunder took the court in their first season wearing team colors of orange-red, white, and two shades of blue. Orange-red mixed the school colors of Oklahoma State University and the University of Oklahoma. Their football teams are the most popular in the state.

The Thunder wear white uniforms at home, with lettering that spells out *THUNDER*. They wear dark blue on the road, with lettering that spells out *OKLAHOMA CITY*. The team's *logo* shows a shield with the letters *OKC*, which is short for "Oklahoma City."

When the Sonics played in Seattle, their colors were green, gold, and white. During the 1990s, the team added red as a uniform color for a few years. The name "SuperSonics" recognized the businesses in the Pacific Northwest that helped build military jets. Supersonic means faster than the speed of sound.

LUCIUS ALLEN
guard

SEATTLE

Lucius Allen models the Sonics' team colors from the 1960s.

14

UNIFORM BASICS

The basketball uniform is very simple. It consists of a roomy top and baggy shorts.

- The top hangs from the shoulders, with big "scoops" for the arms and neck. This style has not changed much over the years.

- Shorts, however, have changed a lot. They used to be very short, so players could move their legs freely. In the last 20 years, shorts have gotten longer and much baggier.

Basketball uniforms look the same as they did long ago ... until you look very closely. In the old days, the shorts had belts and buckles. The tops were made of a thick cotton called "jersey," which got very heavy when players sweated. Later, uniforms were made of shiny *satin*. They may have looked great, but they did not "breathe." As a result, players got very hot! Today, most uniforms are made of *synthetic* materials that soak up sweat and keep the body cool.

Earl Watson wears the Thunder's road uniform during a 2008–09 game.

We Won!

The Sonics went all the way to the NBA Finals in 1977–78, but they lost to the Washington Bullets. Seattle forward Paul Silas looked on the bright side. He said that losing the series would help the young team in the future. Little did Seattle fans realize that the future would arrive exactly one year later. The Sonics and Bullets met again to decide the 1978–79 NBA Championship.

The Sonics had great depth at every position. Their three guards—Gus Williams, Dennis Johnson, and Fred Brown—were brilliant at both ends of the court. The team's front line included Silas along with forwards John Johnson and Lonnie Shelton. When center Jack Sikma needed a break, the *burly* Shelton moved over to take his place.

With coach Lenny Wilkens calling the plays, the Sonics returned to the NBA Finals by defeating the Los Angeles Lakers and Phoenix Suns in the playoffs. The Suns put a scare into the Sonics in the **Western Conference Finals**. The Sonics led the series, but Phoenix won Game 6 at home, 106–105. The Sonics finished off the Suns back in Seattle in another close game, 114–110.

The Bullets had an excellent team, too. In fact, their series against the Sonics was their fourth trip to the NBA Finals during the 1970s.

Paul Silas, whose experience and leadership helped the Sonics win their first NBA Championship.

Their leaders were Wes Unseld, Bob Dandridge, and Elvin Hayes. In Game 1 of the 1979 NBA Finals, backup guard Larry Wright surprised the Sonics. He scored 26 points to help the Bullets win 99–97. Washington held an 18-point lead in the fourth quarter, but the Sonics played with great confidence and nearly pulled out a victory.

That confidence showed in Game 2, even after the Bullets built another lead. This time Seattle did not wait for the fourth quarter to mount a *comeback*. They held the Bullets to just 30 points in the second half and won 92–82. Williams and Dennis Johnson were the stars of the game. The Seattle guards were even better in Game 3. Williams, Johnson, and Brown bombed away and combined for 64 points. The Sonics took the series lead with a 105–95 victory.

Game 4 was a thrilling contest. After four quarters, the score was tied at 104–104. Sikma was *sensational* for the Sonics. He swatted away three shots in the final moments of the fourth period. Seattle outscored the Bullets in **overtime** for a 114–112 victory.

The Sonics were now feeling *unbeatable*. In Game 5, the Seattle guards went wild again. Williams scored 23 points—the fifth game in a row he topped the team in scoring. The Sonics won 97–93 to give Seattle its first major sports championship in more than 60 years.

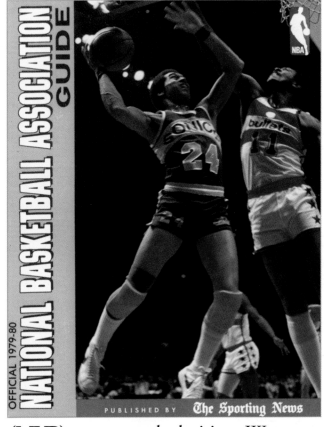

When the series was over, naming the **Most Valuable Player (MVP)** was a tough decision. Was it Williams for his points? Or maybe Sikma for his rebounding? In the end, the trophy went to Dennis Johnson. He averaged 22 points and six **assists** per game. "DJ" also played great defense. He blocked 15 shots and had 19 steals.

LEFT: Gus Williams glides for a layup against the Washington Bullets.
ABOVE: With his MVP performance against the Bullets, Dennis Johnson became the "cover boy" for the 1979–80 NBA Guide.

Go-To Guys

To be a true star in the NBA, you need more than a great shot. You have to be a "go-to guy"—someone teammates trust to make the winning play when the seconds are ticking away in a big game. Fans of the Sonics and Thunder have had a lot to cheer about over the years, including these great stars …

THE PIONEERS

LENNY WILKENS   6´ 1˝ Guard

• BORN: 10/28/1937   • PLAYED FOR TEAM: 1968–69 TO 1971–72

SPENCER HAYWOOD
SUPER SONICS' FORWARD

Lenny Wilkens gave the Sonics an **experienced** leader in their early years. He led the NBA in assists twice. In both of those seasons, he was also Seattle's player-coach!

SPENCER HAYWOOD   6´ 9˝ Forward

• BORN: 4/22/1949

• PLAYED FOR TEAM: 1970–71 TO 1974–75

Spencer Haywood was the top prize in the battle between the NBA and ABA. He joined the Sonics after a long legal fight. In Haywood's third year with the team, he averaged 29 points and nearly 13 rebounds a game. When the club moved to Oklahoma City, those were still team records.

20

ABOVE: Spencer Haywood   **RIGHT**: Gus Williams

FRED BROWN　　　　　　　　　　　　　　　6´ 3˝ **Guard**

- Born: 8/7/1948　　• Played for Team: 1971–72 to 1983–84

Fred Brown played every minute of his 13-year pro career in Seattle. He had one of the NBA's best outside shots. Brown's nickname was "Downtown," because he liked to launch shots far from the basket, which NBA players joked was "downtown."

DENNIS JOHNSON　　　　6´ 4˝ **Guard**

- Born: 9/18/1954　　• Died: 2/22/2007
- Played for Team: 1976–77 to 1979–80

Dennis Johnson was an aggressive player on offense and defense. The day he won a starting job marked the beginning of Seattle's run to the NBA Championship. "DJ" was an All-Star twice with the Sonics.

GUS WILLIAMS　　　　6´ 2˝ **Guard**

- Born: 10/10/1953
- Played for Team: 1977–78 to 1983–84

Gus Williams was called the "Wizard" for the things he could do with a basketball. Williams was as proud as he was talented. He sat out the entire 1980–81 season when he felt Seattle was treating him unfairly.

JACK SIKMA　　　　　　　　　　　　　　6´ 11˝ **Center**

- Born: 11/14/1955　　• Played for Team: 1977–78 to 1985–86

Jack Sikma was a great rebounder and defender. He was also a good shooter—especially from the foul line. Sikma helped the Sonics reach the NBA Finals in each of his first two seasons. He retired with Seattle's team records for rebounds and free throws made.

DALE ELLIS
6′ 7″ Guard/Forward

- BORN: 8/6/1960
- PLAYED FOR TEAM: 1986–87 TO 1990–91 & 1997–98 TO 1998–99

Dale Ellis was an amazing long-distance shooter. He could catch a pass and immediately rise for his jump shot, which gave his defender no time to block it. Ellis averaged more than 20 points per game in each of his first four years with the team.

SHAWN KEMP
6′ 10″ Forward

- BORN: 11/26/1969
- PLAYED FOR TEAM: 1989–90 TO 1996–97

Shawn Kemp was just 20 when he joined the Sonics. His strength and leaping ability made him one of the most exciting players in the NBA. Kemp's favorite play was the alley-oop dunk.

GARY PAYTON
6′ 4″ Guard

- BORN: 7/23/1968
- PLAYED FOR TEAM: 1990–91 TO 2002–03

Gary Payton was known as the "Glove" because he covered his man so tightly. The fast-talking Payton could also dribble, pass, and shoot. He was an excellent leader and a terrific all-around player.

RAY ALLEN 6´5″ **Guard**

• BORN: 7/20/1975 • PLAYED FOR TEAM: 2002–03 TO 2006–07

Ray Allen continued Seattle's *tradition* of guards with a deadly scoring touch. He was one of the league's best scorers and an amazing shooter from beyond the **3-point line**. Allen was named to the **All-NBA** team after the 2003–04 season.

KEVIN DURANT 6´9″ **Forward**

• BORN: 9/29/1988

• FIRST SEASON WITH TEAM: 2007–08

Kevin Durant was the second player chosen in the 2007 draft. Fans marveled at his ability to shoot, dribble, and rebound. By the end of his second season, Durant was being called the first great player in the history of the Thunder.

JEFF GREEN 6´9″ **Forward**

• BORN: 8/28/1986

• FIRST SEASON WITH TEAM: 2007–08

The Thunder got Jeff Green in a trade for Ray Allen. He blossomed in his second season. He and Kevin Durant gave the team the best young forward duo in the NBA.

LEFT: Dale Ellis
ABOVE: Kevin Durant

On the Sidelines

There are many traditions that Oklahoma City fans hope to continue from the club's days in Seattle. Among them is team leadership. The Sonics had some of the best coaches in NBA history. Lenny Wilkens joined the team in 1968–69 as a player and became the player-coach the following season. He led the team to its first winning record. Seattle fans were thrilled when Wilkens returned to the sidelines in 1977–78. He guided the team to the NBA Finals two years in a row.

Over the next few **decades**, the Sonics hired other former players to coach the team. Nate McMillan led the club in the early years of the 21st **century**. He was followed by Bob Weiss, a member of the original Seattle club from 1967–68.

Other coaches who helped mold Seattle into a winner were Bernie Bickerstaff and George Karl. Bickerstaff was very good at working with young players. He rebuilt the Sonics in the 1980s and led them to the Western Conference Finals in 1986–87. Karl got the team to within two victories of a second NBA championship. In each of his seven seasons with the Sonics, they went to the playoffs.

Lenny Wilkens gives his players instructions during a game in the late 1970s.

One Great Day

Basketball fans who attend the NBA All-Star Game also get a glimpse into the future during the Rookie-Sophomore Game. In this contest, a team of first-year players (rookies) faces a team of second-year players (sophomores). Fans watching the 2009 game saw the Thunder's future when Kevin Durant got hot—and stayed hot for 48 minutes.

Durant starred for the Sophomores. He made jump shots, layups, 3-pointers, and dunks on his way to 46 points. That broke the game's old record of 36 points. Durant also had seven rebounds, four assists, and two steals. He made 17 of the 25 shots he took. At times, he was unstoppable.

The Sophomores needed every point, rebound, assist, and steal from Durant. The

LEFT: Kevin Durant dunks during the 2009 Rookie–Sophomore Game.
RIGHT: Durant shares a laugh with Michael Beasley during the game.

Rookies trailed by just three points late in the game. Durant got the ball and drew a foul. He made both of his free throws. The Sophomores pulled out the victory, 122–116.

What made this day extra-special for Durant was that the top scorer for the rookies was Michael Beasley of the Miami Heat. Durant and Beasley had been boyhood friends in Washington, D.C. Getting the best of his longtime buddy was the perfect ending to a perfect day for Durant.

Legend Has It

Which basketball player beat the NBA in the U.S. Supreme Court?

LEGEND HAS IT that Spencer Haywood did. Haywood became a member of the Sonics when he was 21 years old. Back then, the NBA had a rule that prevented players his age or younger from joining the league. Haywood was one of many who did not think this rule was fair. He sued the league, and the case went to the highest court in the land. The Supreme Court decided in Haywood's favor by a vote of 7 to 2. After that, many more young players jumped straight to the NBA from high school.

ABOVE: Lawyer Al Ross, Sonics owner Sam Schulman, and Spencer Haywood celebrate a court victory.
RIGHT: Rashard Lewis, who was named after a pro football star.

Which Sonic was named after a famous football player?

LEGEND HAS IT that Rashard Lewis was. Lewis's mother was a fan of Ahmad Rashad, a football star in the late 1970s. When her son was born, she named him after Rashad—who just happened to be an excellent basketball player, too. The Sonics drafted Lewis in 1998, and he developed into one of the team's top stars. As for the difference in spelling between Rashad and Rashard, Lewis's mom says, "I put a little flavor on the end of it!"

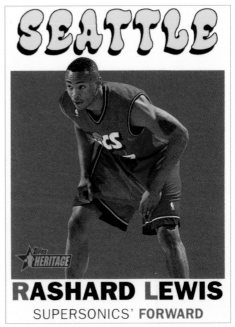

RASHARD LEWIS
SUPERSONICS' **FORWARD**

Who has the biggest wingspan on the Thunder?

LEGEND HAS IT that Kevin Durant does. When most people stand with their arms spread wide, the distance from fingertip to fingertip is usually very close to their height. Durant is 6′ 9″. When he stands with his arms spread, the distance is almost 7′ 5″—or greater than two of the NBA's top centers, Dwight Howard and Greg Oden.

It Really Happened

The Sonics enjoyed their first winning season in 1971–72. They had been in the NBA for just five years. That season, Seattle appeared to be on its way to its first division title. Fans could hardly wait for the playoffs to begin.

Late in the year, the Atlanta Hawks came to town for a game on

a rainy, windy night. The Sonics were on a roll. They had won 12 of their last 14 games.

In Seattle, which is famous for its wet weather, the first thing a basketball team needs is an arena with a good roof. This was not the case with the Seattle Center Coliseum. During the game against the Hawks, dribbles of water splashed to the floor faster than the towel boys could mop them up.

The players were careful to avoid the damp spots, but two of Seattle's stars—Spencer Haywood and Dick Snyder—slipped and fell. Their injuries caused them to miss the remainder of the season. Although the team beat the Hawks that night, they had lost something far greater. Seattle dropped eight of its final nine games and missed the playoffs!

The Sonics had to deal with a leaky roof again more than a decade later. In January of 1986, Seattle was set to host the Phoenix Suns. Once again, the weather was bad, and drops of water fell on the court. This time, the game was called. Today, players from both teams can say they were part of the NBA's first rainout!

SEATTLE SUPER SONICS

$1.00

OFFICIAL 1972-73 PRESS, RADIO, TELEVISION GUIDE

LEFT: A souvenir postcard of the Seattle Center Coliseum.
ABOVE: Spencer Haywood appears on the cover of the team's 1972–73 media guide. He is shown dunking before his injury the previous season.

Team Spirit

Oklahoma City has its own NBA team *because* of team spirit. After Hurricane Katrina struck New Orleans in 2005, the Hornets made their home in Oklahoma City for two seasons. The fans filled the arena night after night to show that they were ready to support a big-league team. When the Hornets returned to their home, the Sonics decided to move to Oklahoma City.

Besides rooting for the Thunder, Oklahoma City fans also cheer for the Thunder Girls dance team. They perform for the crowd during timeouts. During its days in Seattle, the team had two famous *mascots*. The Wheedle was an owl-like creature from a children's book. A larger-than-life Wheedle roamed the sidelines in Seattle during the 1970s and 1980s.

Starting in the 1990s, the team's mascot was named Squatch. Squatch was short for Sasquatch, which is another name for Bigfoot, the legendary beast that some say roams the Pacific Northwest. In 2007, Squatch amazed fans by jumping 30 feet on inline skates—over the cars of Seattle players Ray Allen and Robert Swift.

Team spirit is the reason why Oklahoma City has its own NBA team.

Timeline

The basketball season is played from October through June. That means each season takes place at the end of one year and the beginning of the next. In this timeline, the accomplishments of the Sonics and Thunder are shown by season.

1969–70
Lenny Wilkens leads the NBA in assists.

1973–74
Fred Brown scores 58 points in a game.

1967–68
The Sonics play their first NBA season.

1975–76
"Slick" Watts leads the NBA in steals.

1978–79
The Sonics win the NBA Championship.

Donald "Slick" Watts

Fred Brown

Detlef Schrempf, a star on the 1995–96 team.

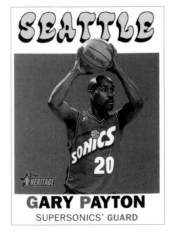

Gary Payton

GARY PAYTON
SUPERSONICS' GUARD

1988–89
Dale Ellis sets a team record with 2,253 points.

1995–96
The Sonics return to the NBA Finals.

1997–98
Gary Payton is voted First Team All-NBA.

1981–82
Jack Sikma sets a team record with 1,038 rebounds.

1991–92
Dana Barros is the league's top 3-point shooter.

2008–09
The Thunder play their first season in Oklahoma City.

Dana Barros

Fun Facts

TRIPLE THREAT

In 2005–06, Ray Allen broke the NBA mark for 3-pointers in a season. He finished the year with 269.

GOING GREEN

When the Sonics left Seattle, owner Clay Bennett agreed to give up the name "SuperSonics" and the team colors of green, white, and gold. NBA **Commissioner** David Stern promised that the NBA would one day put a new team in the city.

SOUNDS LIKE A WINNER

The name "Thunder" makes basketball fans think of the state's famous storms. However, it also honors Oklahoma's Native American *folklore* and traditions. Thunder plays an important role in the history of that culture.

ABOVE: Ray Allen waves to the Seattle fans after setting the record for 3-pointers in one season.
RIGHT: Wally Walker, who was known as "Wally Wonder."

WONDER BOY

Wally Walker was a fan favorite for the Sonics. He was a part of the three Seattle teams that won Western Conference championships— twice as a player and once as a team *executive*. During his playing days, Walker was nicknamed "Wally Wonder."

CRAZY LIKE A FOX

Some fans thought the Sonics were crazy when they traded hot-shooting Don Kojis for center Jim Fox in 1972. That December, Fox set a team record with 30 rebounds in a game.

RUB OUT

During the 1977–78 season, center Marvin Webster blocked 162 shots and grabbed 1,035 rebounds. Seattle fans called him the "Human Eraser" because he made so many shots "disappear."

CHECK THE LABEL

In a 1989 game against the Houston Rockets, Avery Johnson took the court with his shorts inside out. This is against the rules. His teammates had to form a human wall around him so he could change.

Talking Hoops

"I don't talk trash. I just go out there and have fun."

—Kevin Durant, on the right way to play

"The most important thing in winning basketball games is **chemistry**."

—Shawn Kemp, on the secret to success in the NBA

"I really believe defense is an art."

—Dennis Johnson, on what made him a great player

"If you believe you can do something, don't let anybody in the whole world tell you that you can't."

—"Slick" Watts, on the importance of self-confidence

"If you want to be a great shooter, you have to shoot the same way every time."

—Ray Allen, on learning to be consistent

ABOVE: Shawn Kemp   **RIGHT**: Gary Payton

"We were the ones who started that alley-oop and lob stuff, and got really good at it."

—*Gary Payton, on his teamwork with Shawn Kemp*

"The real superstar was a man or a woman raising six kids on $150 a week."

—*Spencer Haywood, on who he looked up to during his career*

"Creating a **dilemma** for the defense is what **playmaking** is all about."

—*Walt Hazzard, on his philosophy on offense*

"This is heaven for me."

—*Fred Brown, on winning the 1978–79 NBA Championship*

For the Record

T he great Sonics and Thunder teams and players have left their marks on the record books. These are the "best of the best" …

Gary Payton

SONICS AND THUNDER AWARD WINNERS

WINNER	AWARD	SEASON
Lenny Wilkens	All-Star Game MVP	1970–71
Dennis Johnson	NBA Finals MVP	1978–79
Tom Chambers	All-Star Game MVP	1986–87
Dale Ellis	Most Improved Player	1986–87
Dale Ellis	3-Point Shootout Champion	1988–89
Gary Payton	Defensive Player of the Year	1995–96
Desmond Mason	NBA Slam Dunk Champion	2000–01
Kevin Durant	Rookie of the Year	2007–08

Kevin Durant

Desmond Mason during the 2001 Slam Dunk Contest.

SONICS AND THUNDER ACHIEVEMENTS

ACHIEVEMENT	SEASON
Western Conference Champions	1977–78
Pacific Division Champions	1978–79
Western Conference Champions	1978–79
NBA Champions	1978–79
Pacific Division Champions	1993–94
Pacific Division Champions	1995–96
Western Conference Champions	1995–96
Pacific Division Champions	1996–97
Pacific Division Champions	1997–98
Northwest Division Champions	2004–05

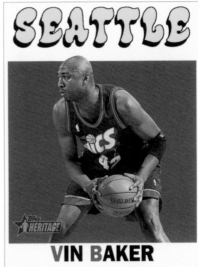

VIN BAKER
SUPERSONICS' FORWARD

TOP: Vin Baker, a star for the 1997–98 team.
ABOVE: Vladimir Radmanovic, a star for the 2004–05 team.
LEFT: Tom Chambers, the 1987 All-Star Game MVP.

41

Pinpoints

The history of a basketball team is made up of many smaller stories. These stories take place all over the map—not just in the city a team calls "home." Match the pushpins on these maps to the Team Facts and you will begin to see the story of the Sonics and Thunder unfold!

TEAM FACTS

1 Oklahoma City, Oklahoma—*The Thunder played their first season here in 2008–09.*

2 Kankakee, Illinois—*Jack Sikma was born here.*

3 Elkhart, Indiana—*Shawn Kemp was born here.*

4 Penn Hills, Pennsylvania—*George Karl was born here.*

5 Brooklyn, New York—*Lenny Wilkens was born here.*

6 Cheverly, Maryland—*Jeff Green was born here.*

7 Pineville, Louisiana—*Rashard Lewis was born here.*

8 Silver City, Mississippi—*Spencer Haywood was born here.*

9 Milwaukee, Wisconsin—*Fred Brown was born here.*

10 Oakland, California—*Gary Payton was born here.*

11 Seattle, Washington—*The Sonics played here from 1967–68 to 2007–08.*

12 Leverkusen, Germany—*Detlef Schrempf was born here.*

Jeff Green

43

Play Ball

Basketball is a sport played by two teams of five players. NBA games have four 12-minute quarters—48 minutes in all—and the team that scores the most points when time has run out is the winner. Most baskets count for two points. Players who make shots from beyond the three-point line receive an extra point. Baskets made from the free-throw line count for one point. Free throws are penalty shots awarded to a team, usually after an opponent has committed a foul. A foul is called when one player makes hard contact with another.

Players can move around all they want, but the player with the ball cannot. He must bounce the ball with one hand or the other (but never both) in order to go from one part of the court to another. As long as he keeps "dribbling," he can keep moving.

In the NBA, teams must attempt a shot every 24 seconds, so there is little time to waste. The job of the defense is to make it as difficult as possible for the offense to take a good shot—and to grab the ball if the other team shoots and misses.

This may sound simple, but anyone who has played the game knows that basketball can be very complicated. Every player on the court has a job to do. Different players have different strengths and weaknesses. The coach must mix these players in just the right way and teach them to work together as one.

The more you play and watch basketball, the more "little things" you are likely to notice. The next time you watch a game, look for these plays:

PLAY LIST

ALLEY-OOP—A play in which the passer throws the ball just to the side of the rim—so a teammate can catch it and dunk in one motion.

BACK-DOOR PLAY—A play in which the passer waits for a teammate to fake the defender away from the basket—then throws him the ball when he cuts back toward the basket.

KICK-OUT—A play in which the ball handler waits for the defense to surround him—then quickly passes to a teammate who is open for an outside shot. The ball is not really kicked in this play; the term comes from the action of pinball machines.

NO-LOOK PASS—A play in which a passer fools the defense by looking in one direction, then making a surprise pass to a teammate.

PICK-AND-ROLL—A play in which one player blocks, or "picks off," a teammate's defender with his body, then in the confusion cuts to the basket for a pass.

Glossary

BASKETBALL WORDS TO KNOW

3-POINT LINE—The line on the court that separates 2-point baskets from 3-point baskets. A shot made from behind this line is worth three points.

ALL-AROUND—Good at all parts of the game.

ALL-NBA—An honor given at the end of the season to the NBA's best players at each position.

ALL-STAR—A player selected to play in the annual All-Star Game.

AMERICAN BASKETBALL ASSOCIATION (ABA)—The basketball league that played for nine seasons starting in 1967. Prior to the 1976–77 season, four ABA teams joined the NBA, and the rest went out of business.

ASSISTS—Passes that lead to successful shots.

CHEMISTRY—The way players work together on and off the court. Winning teams usually have good chemistry.

COMMISSIONER—The person in charge of a professional sports league.

DRAFTED—Chosen from a group of the best college players. The NBA draft is held each summer.

HALL OF FAMER—A player who has been honored as being among the greatest ever and is enshrined in the Basketball Hall of Fame.

LINEUP—The list of players who are playing in a game.

MOST VALUABLE PLAYER (MVP)—The award given each year to the league's best player; also given to the best player in the league finals and All-Star Game.

NATIONAL BASKETBALL ASSOCIATION (NBA)—The professional league that has been operating since 1946–47.

NBA FINALS—The playoff series that decides the champion of the league.

NORTHWEST DIVISION—A group of teams that play in the northwest part of the country.

OVERTIME—The extra period played when a game is tied after 48 minutes.

PACIFIC DIVISION—A group of teams that play in a region that is close to the Pacific Ocean.

PLAYER-COACH—A person who plays for a team and coaches it at the same time.

PLAYMAKING—Creating scoring opportunities.

PLAYOFFS—The games played after the season to determine the league champion.

PROFESSIONAL—A player or team that plays a sport for money.

ROLE PLAYERS—People who are asked to do specific things when they are in a game.

ROOKIE OF THE YEAR—The annual award given to the league's best first-year player.

ROSTER—The list of players on a team.

WESTERN CONFERENCE FINALS—The playoff series that determines which team from the West will play the best team in the East for the NBA Championship.

OTHER WORDS TO KNOW

BURLY—Having a large, strong body.

CENTURY—A period of 100 years.

COMEBACK—The process of catching up from behind, or making up a large deficit.

DECADES—Periods of 10 years; also specific periods, such as the 1950s.

DILEMMA—A very tricky problem.

EXECUTIVE—A person who makes important decisions for a company.

EXPERIENCED—Having knowledge and skill in a job.

FOLKLORE—Customs, tales, sayings, dances, or art forms preserved among a group of people.

LOGO——A symbol or design that represents a company or team.

MASCOTS—Animals or people believed to bring a group good luck.

MERGED—Joined forces.

SATIN—A smooth, shiny fabric.

SENSATIONAL—Amazing.

SYNTHETIC—Made in a laboratory, not in nature.

TRADITION—A belief or custom that is handed down from generation to generation.

UNBEATABLE—Impossible to defeat.

Places to Go

ON THE ROAD

OKLAHOMA CITY THUNDER
100 West Reno Avenue
Oklahoma City, Oklahoma 73102
(405) 208-4800

NAISMITH MEMORIAL BASKETBALL HALL OF FAME
1000 West Columbus Avenue
Springfield, Massachusetts 01105
(877) 4HOOPLA

ON THE WEB

THE NATIONAL BASKETBALL ASSOCIATION   www.nba.com
  • *Learn more about the league's teams, players, and history*

THE OKLAHOMA CITY THUNDER   www.nba.com/thunder
  • *Learn more about the Thunder*

THE BASKETBALL HALL OF FAME   www.hoophall.com
  • *Learn more about history's greatest players*

ON THE BOOKSHELF

To learn more about the sport of basketball, look for these books at your library or bookstore:

  • Stewart, Mark and Kennedy, Mike. *Swish: the Quest for Basketball's Perfect Shot.* Minneapolis, Minnesota: Millbrook Press, 2009.
  • Ramen, Fred. *Basketball: Rules, Tips, Strategy & Safety.* New York, New York: Rosen Central, 2007.
  • Labrecque, Ellen. *Basketball.* Ann Arbor, Michigan: Cherry Lake Publishing, 2009.
  • Wyckoff, Edwin Brit. *The Man Who Invented Basketball: James Naismith and His Amazing Game.* Berkeley Heights, New Jersey: Enslow Elementary, 2008.

Index

The Team

MARK STEWART has written more than 20 books on basketball, and over 100 sports books for kids. He grew up in New York City during the 1960s rooting for the Knicks and Nets, and now takes his two daughters, Mariah and Rachel, to watch them play. Mark comes from a family of writers. His grandfather was Sunday Editor of *The New York Times* and his mother was Articles Editor of *The Ladies Home Journal* and *McCall's*. Mark has profiled hundreds of athletes over the last 20 years. He has also written several books about his native New York, and New Jersey, his home today. Mark is a graduate of Duke University, with a degree in history. He lives with his daughters and wife, Sarah, overlooking Sandy Hook, New Jersey.

MATT ZEYSING is the resident historian at the Basketball Hall of Fame in Springfield, Massachusetts. His research interests include the origins of the game of basketball, the development of professional basketball in the first half of the 20th century, and the culture and meaning of basketball in American society.